7.50
C3
D

13675

THE CALL OF THE MOUNTAINS

THE CALL OF THE MOUNTAINS

COLIN WYATT

WITH
75 PHOTOGRAVURE PLATES

THE BEECHHURST PRESS · NEW YORK

To my Father
JAMES WILLIAM WYATT

FIRST AMERICAN EDITION 1953
PUBLISHED BY THE BEECHHURST PRESS, NEW YORK
PRINTED IN GREAT BRITAIN

CONTENTS

PLATES

PREAMBLE

MOST OF my life has been spent among mountains—walking over the flower-covered alps of Central Europe and Canada, riding through the passes that pierce the limestone peaks of Albania or ski-ing across the frozen rivers and lakes of Lapland, among the golden birches. Snow is my greatest delight—its glorious soft shadows, its infinite variety of texture and the stories that the beasts and birds write on it with their tracks. Above all, I love ski-ing among the solitudes of the glaciers—in that remote world of glittering peaks and luminous shadows on hanging faces of ice where knife-sharp snow arêtes seem to cut into the dome of heaven itself.

For me the mountains are not merely a challenge to technical skill, human endurance and strength of will, not just varying arrangements of different geological structures, but definite and complex entities each with a distinctive character and endowed with an almost infinite variety of moods. The character of a mountain does not just consist of the quality and arrangement of its rocks and glaciers, but of the flowers that grow on its upper pastures, the animals in the forests that clothe its flanks, and the character and culture of the peasants who dwell in the valleys around its base.

Once I had had my initial fill of the pleasures of conquering rock and ice, the sensuous joys of warm stone under my hands in summer and the velvet hiss of glacier snows beneath my ski in winter, I began to want to know more about the more living aspect of the mountains, about their history and the sort of people and animals who live among them.

My father was lucky enough to have known the Alps of Switzerland and Austria in the "golden age" of climbing, before the tourist industry had been thought of, but I soon found the majority of the central European mountains too much of a beaten highway, too much "developed". Seeking to understand them I had gone back into the classics of alpine literature, to the writings of Whymper and Mummery; after reading the stories of their adventures and explorations I found myself irked by the modern roads, railways, hotels and huts of Switzerland and Austria, although thoroughly appreciating them from the practical point of view when it came to making a purely technical climbing trip. I love the characters and traditions of the present-day peasants of the Alps, but I wanted something more primitive—to try to capture for myself something of the spirit of adventure that my father had experienced seventy years ago; so, whenever opportunity offered, I began to go to out-of-the-way countries and to mountains where very few people had been before.

Some, such as the Jotunheim Mountains in Norway, were still in much the same stage, alpinistically speaking, as were the Swiss Alps in the 1880's, while others were almost completely wild and untouched. Although many of them did not present much in the way of actual physical climbing, they offered true mountaineering in the sense of exploring and getting to know strange mountain peoples and places which twentieth-century civilization had not reached, and it is mostly of these that I write. But the comparison of the mountain ranges of distant lands with the Alps is interesting, and affords a familiar standard by which to measure; so I have included some photographs of the Alps in winter and told of the joys of ski-mountaineering, which is to me the most completely satisfying form of alpinism.

For the rest, I have set out to give an impression of the less-known mountains and their inhabitants, of the Lapps, the peasants of Albania, the Berbers of the High Atlas of Morocco, and of the wilds of New Zealand and Australia.

CHAPTER I

THE SNOWS OF AFRICA

THERE IS great pleasure in achieving the seemingly impossible, and I had long been intrigued with the idea of going ski-ing in Africa. I felt certain that there was good snow in the High Atlas, the great range of mountains—already famed in antiquity—separating the fertile North Moroccan plain from the sands of the Sahara; so a couple of Swiss friends and myself assembled within the red ramparts of Marrakech in March 1949 with a view to finding out.

A burning, almost tropical sun illumined the great square of Djemâa el Fna; around us seethed the throng—hook-nosed Arabs in their long white and brown djellabahs, a great silver dagger on the hip, and mysterious veiled women whose brown eyes gazed aslant at us through their yashmaks. From time to time a camel caravan passed, come from the sands of the South across the cols of the Atlas, the animals navigating the crowd like ships through a choppy sea. A swarthy Arab loaded the last case on our lorry and piled the ski, rucksacks and ice-axes on top. A long blast on the horn and we were off . . . behind us the throb of the snake-charmer's tom-toms slowly died away and five minutes later we left the city under the great arch of the South Gate. Beyond the many-coloured plain rose the gleaming white chain of the High Atlas, filling the whole horizon.

The road led across pink fields of wild gladioli splashed with the gold of Adonis anemones and the white of daisies; every now and again we passed a village whose flat-topped houses of red pisé hid behind walls of blue-green cactus. Soon we were at 4,000 feet among the olive groves and barley fields of Asni; its red houses, dominated by the great fortress of the Caïd, terraced the west flank of a wild valley whose slopes, blue with lavender, framed the snows of the majestic Toubkal, 13,744 feet, the highest mountain in North Africa.

The village headman led us to his house and regaled us with mint-tea and a mutton stew; this we ate with our fingers, sitting cross-legged on mats. Having noisily indicated our satisfaction and repletion in the local manner, we started bargaining for pack-mules so that we should be ready to set off at dawn on the morrow.

Most of the villagers assembled to see us off. The headman offered us a farewell round of mint-tea, and then the caravan wound its way through the narrow alleys of the village on to the sunny slopes above, where the track led through innumerable clumps of giant asphodels whose white stars stood out sharply against the deep blue of the valley shadows. For four hours we ascended the valley of the Ait Mizane. Now and then the valley widened into a bright green chequer-board of young barley fields, divided by walls of white stones; a few scrawny cows pastured by the side of the torrent, tended by Berber women clad in rich orange robes. Occasionally, perched on a spur, the grim walls of a castellated Kasbah guarded the track like a mediaeval fortress, and flat-roofed red villages clung to the steep hillsides. Suddenly our muleteers began a strange, oriental song—sometimes one voice, sometimes in chorus—a weird refrain repeated again and again in variations of a minor key. Apart from that, not a sound could be heard beyond the roar of the torrent and the dull blows of a stick on the rump of a recalcitrant mule.

At noon we arrived at Imelil, the last village, nestling in still-leafless walnut groves, where the village grocer gave us mint-tea. Rested and refreshed we came to the Plain of Arround, right at the foot of the Toubkal, a flat sea of purple moraine and huge boulders that forms one of the few remnants of the ancient glaciers. We were now at 6,600 feet, and the track climbed steeply in zigzags up a slope dotted with thuriferous junipers, the characteristic high alpine tree of the Atlas, large and aromatic and very like the Arolla pine of the Alps.

Soon the first patch of snow appeared, and a moment later we found the track blocked by a huge drift. The leading mule refused to set foot on it, and we had to form in line and stamp out a firm trail and then cajole it carefully across with two Berbers supporting it below. A mile or so beyond, the whole valley was white—we had reached the snow-line at 9,500 feet. Here we dumped our cases and the muleteers took their beasts back to Asni, leaving us with four specially selected porters, real hardy mountaineers, whom we had engaged at Imelil. We left one man to guard the depot, while the other three began a shuttle service to a small hut, built by the French Alpine Club, now only about an hour away.

What a pleasure to set ski on African snow for the first time! The skins slid along over a perfect spring snow across wonderful ski slopes towards a white pass on the sky-line. On our left rose the cliffs of the vast north face of the Toubkal, cut by a sinister couloir 3,000 feet high from which emerged the débris of a gigantic avalanche, while to our right the jagged peaks of the Ouanoukrim Range stood out against the blue sky.

Next day we rolled out of our sleeping-bags at dawn; while the porters started digging for water in the creek, ten feet down under the snow, Edmond and I set off on ski up the narrow valley. Seven hundred feet higher it widened; we turned right, crossing the fresh track of a jackal, and climbed up a snow-filled defile which debouched into an enormous amphitheatre, a real skier's paradise rejoicing in the name of the Amrharhas n'Iglioua. At 12,680 feet, on a little col at its head, we deposited our ski and roped up for the final climb to the top of the Afella n'Ouanoukrim. At the start all went well, but we soon arrived at the foot of a shady couloir where the rocks were badly iced and every hold had to be cleaned with the ice-axe. Then came some steep step-cutting in solidly frozen snow, and after 700 feet of trying work we at last came into the sun again on a narrow ridge. From one step to the next the snow became soft and the heat almost insupportable—it was past 11 a.m. But we were not the only living beings up here: the fresh tracks of a mouflon, the wild bighorn sheep of the Atlas—coming from goodness knows where—led us up the snow and rock ridge to the summit, 13,342 feet. Opposite rose the imposing mass of the Toubkal, just overtopping us, while beyond the southern slopes of the Atlas, like a red sea at the foot of white cliffs, spread a labyrinth of arid valleys and rocky escarpments that lost themselves in the shimmer of distant sands. One solitary mountain stood out like a pearl against a background of copper, the Siroua, 10,900 feet, the only snow peak of the Anti-Atlas. To the north, the jagged rock ridge of the Ouanoukrim Range sloped down towards the blue-violet haze of the Moroccan plain.

The snow was soft in the couloir when we descended and we had to take great care, for below was just an abyss. On the rocks it went faster and we were soon back at our ski; a short rest, a bite of chocolate, and we launched ourselves down the slope. The snow was superb, and soon the christies interlaced from top to bottom of the amphitheatre, the tracks uniting in the valley in a long schuss that took us almost back to the hut door. After a good meal we took a sun-bath in front of the hut, lulled by the chirping of the choughs; a lump of snow fell from the top of a rock with a dull thud—were we really in Africa?

The next day marked the culminating point of the expedition, for at 7 a.m. we left the hut for the Toubkal, taking the route up the sharply rising valley immediately opposite. The steep slopes were frozen so solid that neither seal-skins nor steel edges would bite, and we had to put on crampons and carry ski for 300 feet to the more gradual valley above. Then a very pleasant climb brought us out into a basin immediately under the west face, whence we had the choice of two alternatives, either to ski up to the base of the South Ridge, or to the opposite Northwest Ridge. The latter looked more promising and would be more sheltered, for a strong wind had got up. At last we reached the rocks of the ridge and planted our ski deep in the snow in the lee of a rock; from there on it was just a long scramble over rock and ice to the little summit plateau at 13,744 feet. The view was quite indescribable; it seemed as if the whole of the High Atlas and all Morocco was spread out around us—Edmond even swore he could see the Canary Islands off the Atlantic Coast!

We were now above the wind, and hated to tear ourselves away; but if we were to delay much longer the snow would become too soft for good ski-ing, and so at 11 a.m. we turned back down the ridge. The snow was just right; we spun down in long christies to the basin, and it was only a moment before we found ourselves on top of the steep slopes opposite the hut. Here the snow was terrifically fast and we arrived only half an hour after leaving the summit;

Brahim and Aomar had spotted us from afar and had a vast platter of couscous, a sort of crushed barley "rice" and mutton, awaiting us.

For the next two days we had more wonderful ski-ing and climbing, but we awoke on the fourth day to hear the wind moaning round the hut. It was the Sirocco, laden with the sand of the Sahara, the Atlas equivalent of the Foehn, and the weather looked bad. However, it was going to be a day of rest anyhow; for on the morrow we proposed to cross the Toubkal Range, the plan being to traverse two rock peaks and descend into a little-known valley beyond, whence we should attack another big snow peak in the Tifnout massif, while our porters with our tents and provisions took a roundabout lower route.

When the alarm went off next day at six o'clock, the gale was blowing outside with undiminished vigour. There was no sign of our porters, due to come up from Imelil to meet us, and anxiously we made coffee. It was nearly 9 a.m. by the time they arrived, frozen and gloomy, having waded through the snow in bare legs and sandals, in the teeth of the gale. We hastened to give them bread and hot coffee, while Robert cajoled and exhorted them; soon their wonted good humour returned and they shook themselves and laughed . . . "Safi! Safi!"—"Okay! Let's go!"

We set off simultaneously, the two porters on foot by the track and we on ski with heavy packs and the sleeping-bags, just in case we did not meet them that night as arranged, for we had started far later than we intended. We skied down the valley for a thousand feet to where it was filled by the huge avalanche débris, and then began a steep climb up the couloir towards the Tizi n'Immouzer, a pass 3,000 feet above. The couloir was barred by three great terraces of rock and blue ice, and in places we had to carry our ski up narrow chimneys and traverse along iced ledges. To make matters worse it began to hail, and pellets the size of peas bounced off the snow all round us. At last we arrived at a little basin at the foot of the last cliffs of the Toubkal, where we were out of the wind; with frozen fingers we fumbled in our rucksacks for a snack, while around us danced the bullets of hail.

The last slope was so steep and icy that our sealskins gripped no longer—cursing under our breath we put on crampons and carried our ski. Finally, after climbing for three and three-quarter hours, we reached the col. The view was incredibly wild, but we had no time to look at it for the wind was almost

7 Moroccan High Atlas — Mt. Aksoual

11 Moroccan High Atlas — Ouaougoulzat Range

m'Goun range was much nearer now and we could pick out the main summit and the way to approach it, though it still looked an awfully long way off. The lower, eastern end of the range was almost opposite to us, and through the deep cleft of a river gorge we could see the red shimmer of the desert far, far away. We made our way back to our ski and then skimmed down for over 3,000 feet on spring snow, descending in a few minutes what had taken us hours to climb.

All next day we trudged down the Ait Bougemmez valley along a hot, stony track, wishing we had light shoes instead of our heavy climbing boots. Every now and then we passed by the walls of fortress villages, and sometimes the four-square castle of some Sheikh would jut out from the mountainside high above us. At about 4 o'clock we came to a very big village, and a messenger came out to say that the Sheikh would like us to take tea with him. We were led down through tunnels in the walls and through huge wooden doors to an inner courtyard where he, his son, and his grand vizier stood awaiting us. He was a wonderful old man with a nose like an eagle's beak, white-bearded but as straight as a die, and a good six feet tall. His robes and turban were of spotless white, and a huge chased-silver dagger hung at his hip from a crimson cord. He led us through cool, whitewashed corridors to a room spread with rich rugs; the walls were painted in geometrical designs of many colours and hung with bright brass and copper utensils. He kicked off his slippers and watched us with amused tolerance as we struggled with the laces of our boots; then an old man brought in a three-foot-high brass brazier and a huge tea-kettle, while another came round with a brass bowl and a carved ewer of water for us to wash our hands. Although we were anxious to get as far as possible before dark we had to be tactful, and so an hour and a half came to be passed in polite conversation before we continued on our way.

That night we slept in comfort in yet another village, and at dawn we set off up a side valley, which led us to high alpine pastures where the puddles were glazed with ice. A dignified horseman on a high-pommeled, brightly embroidered saddle was watching a peasant ploughing the first furrow of spring, and there was a tang in the air that reminded me of Switzerland. Ahead, the triple peak of the m'Goun appeared, framed by a terrific gorge, and it was a great thrill to see our final goal so close. To avoid the gorge, which was